How to

QUINOA

· · · · · · ·

Life Lessons from
My Imaginary
Well-Dressed Daughter

Tiffany Beveridge

RUNNING PRESS
PHILADELPHIA · LONDON

© 2014 by Tiffany Beveridge
Published by Running Press,
A Member of the Perseus Books Group

Printed in the United States

Books published by Running Press are available at special discounts for bulk purchases in the United States by corporations, institutions, and other organizations. For more information, please contact the Special Markets Department at the Perseus Books Group, 2300 Chestnut Street, Suite 200, Philadelphia, PA 19103, or call (800) 810-4145, ext. 5000, or e-mail special.markets@perseusbooks.com.

ISBN 978-0-7624-5427-3
Library of Congress Control Number: 2013958109

E-book ISBN 978-0-7624-5430-3

9   8   7   6   5   4   3   2   1
Digit on the right indicates the number of this printing

Cover and interior design by Ashley Haag
Edited by Jordana Tusman
Typography: Thirsty Rough, Futura, and Sans Serif

Running Press Book Publishers
2300 Chestnut Street
Philadelphia, PA 19103-4371

Visit us on the web!
www.runningpress.com

Contents

Introduction ...5

Chapter 1
THE HIPSTER MOVEMENT EXPLAINED ...7
The Rules of Being a Hipster ...9

Quinoa's Essential Hipster Vocabulary List ...11

The Hipster Hiding in Your Closet (and If Not Yours, Maybe Your Grandpa's) ...16

Chapter 2
PARENTING THE WORLD'S MOST INFLUENTIAL DAUGHTER ...19
Choosing a Quinoa-esque Name ...24

Stuck with a Bad Name? Quinoa's Tips for Choosing an On-Trend Nickname ...27

The Quinoa Method Illustrated ...28

Chapter 3
WELL-DRESSED IS THE SEVEREST OF UNDERSTATEMENTS ...31
WWQW? (What Would Quinoa Wear?) ...38

The Seven Deadly Sins of Fashion 39

Chapter 4
ALL GOOD DESIGNERS LEAD TO HAPPINESS ...41
Finding Your Own Path to Designer Happiness ...49

Quinoa's Patented Textile Cleanse ...50

Chapter 5
INSIDE THE PRESCHOOL YOU'D NEVER OTHERWISE GET INTO ...53
Marketing Yourself for Top Preschools ...62

Ten Buzzwords to Get Your Application Noticed ...63

Chapter 6

EXTRACURRICULARS: THE DIFFERENCE BETWEEN ORDINARY AND EXTRAORDINARY ...65

Piano Lessons Are for Poor Kids ...73

Quinoa's Top Ten Charities ...74

Chapter 7

FOOD FOR THOUGHT: WHY EAT A CARROT WHEN YOU CAN EAT AN ACCESSORY? ...77

Three-Part Series: Munch-Needed Makeover ...80

Part 1: Upgrade and You've Got It Made ...80

Part 2: Hyphenate Your Way to Great ...82

Part 3: Easy to Pronounce? Less Than One Ounce! ...85

Quinoa's Twenty Tips for Improving Your Personal Foodie Status ...89

Chapter 8

QUINOA AND CHEVRON, BEST FRIENDS FOREVER (PROBABLY) ...93

How Does Your BFF Score on a Scale from 1 to Chevron? ...101

Quinoa's Tips for Increasing Your Friendship Drama ...102

Chapter 9

PLAYDATES ARE THE NEW POWER LUNCH ...105

Quinoa's Respectable Elaborate Playdate Themes ...111

When and How to Turn Down a Subpar Invitation ...112

Chapter 10

QUINOA GOES GLOBAL ...115

Quinoa's Standard Packing List ...122

Quinoa's Essential International Phrases ...124

Photo Credits ...126

Acknowledgments ...127

INTRODUCTION

MEET QUINOA. She's the fearless and fashion-forward little girl who dresses to the ninety-nines, attends elaborately themed playdates with her cohort of posh friends like Chevron, Hashtag, and Aioli, and yet still finds time to help orphans and other poorly dressed children. She sets more trends in an hour than the number of times you check your email and Twitter feed.

That viral article you read on BuzzFeed? Quinoa tipped them off to it last week. That new indie band everybody's downloading? Quinoa was their first backer on Kickstarter. That must-have accessory everybody's wearing? Quinoa just donated her gently used one to Goodwill this morning. She's equal parts innovative, inspiring, and ridiculously adorable. It's been said that Quinoa is the Steve Jobs of pop culture, but, in reality, Steve Jobs was the Quinoa of a computer company. She's got more cool factor than all the Kardashian, Jolie-Pitt, and Paltrow offspring combined.

Oh, yeah, she's also imaginary. NBD.

Based on the wildly popular Pinterest board, My Imaginary Well-Dressed Toddler Daughter, this book goes beyond telling you *about* Quinoa. This book will show you *how to* Quinoa. By the time you're done reading, you will be exponentially more interesting and on-trend. You'll dress with conviction and Quinoa's special brand of SHAZAM! You'll eat relevant, on-point foods like chia seeds and kale and other edible accessories. You'll choose better-looking friends (but not better-looking than you). You'll discover the empowering experience of Quinoa's patented textile cleanse (one week of white cotton clothing with the labels cut out).

WELL, STICK A MUSTACHE ON IT AND LIST IT ON ETSY, THAT'S AMAZING!

—QUINOA

You'll book enviable vacations to places poor people can't even pronounce, void of tourists, budgets, or fanny packs. You'll learn the inner workings of the modern power playdate. You'll devote spare time to meaningful causes like Eighties Awareness and Friends of Soy. Eventually, when the time is right, you'll be prepared to produce attractive, well-dressed, appropriately named progeny of your own.

This book is like an ambush makeover from the inside out, setting you on a path to success of the most substantial and photogenic kind. (Plus, the book itself is this season's hottest accessory. All the cool kids are carrying one.)

So before you begin, there's really only one question left:

Are you ready to QUINOA?

Chapter 1

The **HIPSTER MOVEMENT**
EXPLAINED

When it comes to the sensitive topic of hipsters and Quinoa's alleged involvement in the movement, it's important to consider the facts. Quinoa has neither confirmed nor denied her role as the Most High Hipster, though a number of scholars have confidently arrived at that conclusion. All speculation about her role in leading droves of twenty- and thirtysomethings to skinny jeans, handlebar mustache paraphernalia, and independent banjo music is just that—speculation.

The facts are these: While visiting a Brooklyn farmers' market once, baby Quinoa popped the lenses out of her tiny Ray-Ban Wayfarers, put them on, and sipped her vegan alfalfa smoothie. Many a bamboo-clad shopper that day was seen dropping their reusable grocery bags and removing the lenses from their own glasses.

A week later, while visiting Portland, Oregon, Quinoa donned a slouchy cashmere cap, a flannel plaid shirt, and a teething toy in the shape of a tobacco pipe, a gift from a dear family friend in the vinyl record industry. A nearby gathering of underemployed baristas with MFAs holding a support group took notice. (Three of them tweeted about it. Two wrote a haiku.)

Fast-forward three days and Quinoa is spotted in East Austin, Texas, wearing Ikat leggings and a tweed

SOMETIMES QUINOA AND HER BFF CHEVRON LIKE TO JUST SIT ON THE SIDEWALK AND COUNT HOW MANY SECONDS GO BY BETWEEN FOOD TRUCKS.

fedora at a pickle festival. Whether it was planned or not we'll never know, but Quinoa dumped her organic vegetable snack pack into an open jar of pickle juice. Bystanders applauded and immediately began pickling everything in sight.

Were these incidents a deliberate grassroots effort or mere coincidence? Was it written in the stars that these otherwise lost adults should find cultural direction and purpose from an infant holding a vintage Holga camera? When questioned, Quinoa simply shrugged, readjusted her messenger bag, and whistled a little Arcade Fire refrain.

While she denies direct involvement, Quinoa does consider herself a student of hipster culture.

According to Q, there are eight rules of being a hipster:

THE RULES
of being a hipster

1. YOU DO NOT CALL YOURSELF A HIPSTER.
2. *YOU DO NOT CALL YOURSELF A HIPSTER.*
3. IF SOMETHING IS DEEMED "COOL" OR "MAINSTREAM" OR "POPULAR," ITS APPEAL IS IMMEDIATELY OVER.
4. ONLY TWO NECK TATTOOS, TEMPORARY OR OTHERWISE.
5. ONE SCARF AT A TIME, FELLAS.
6. NO WELL-TAILORED SHIRTS, NO CHEAP SHOES (only expensive shoes that look like cheap shoes).
7. IRONY WILL GO ON AS LONG AS IT HAS TO.
8. MUSTACHES. PERIOD.

This secret society with a penchant for music festivals and bow ties seems to have no political aspirations, other than constitutional freedom to worship Bob Ross, patterned socks, Mumford & Sons, and nonprofit organizations without any snickering.

How big is this movement? Quinoa confirms hearing rumors that hipster culture is even bigger than it appears on the surface.

SOMETIMES QUINOA LIKES TO TIE A BALLOON TO HER WRIST, HOP ON HER VESPA, AND DO SOME RANDOM DRIVE-BY HOLGA SHOOTINGS.

SOMETIMES ON AN EARLY SUNDAY MORNING, QUINOA WILL STROLL THE QUIET STREETS, BELTING OUT SOME VINTAGE RADIOHEAD.

QUINOA'S *Essential* HIPSTER *VOCABULARY LIST*

Mainstream – (adjective) *The root of all evil* Barley would rather burn her first-edition autographed copy of *Catcher in the Rye* than be **mainstream**.

Retro – (adjective) *Superior; better than* When asked to describe his Mason jar music, Dakota said it was very **retro**.

On-point – (adjective) *Superior; better than* Jicama found the lecture on organic felted wool soaps to be very **on-point**.

Vintage – (adjective) *Superior; better than* Ombre's housedress made from **vintage** bedsheets was the envy of all the girls at the letterpress class.

Locally sourced – (adjective) *Superior; better than* Beige and Hominy were only interested in adopting a **locally sourced** shelter dog.

Mid-century modern – (adjective) *Superior; better than* Pantone loathed the itchy, boxy orange couch until she discovered it was **mid-century modern**.

Indie – (adjective) *Superior; better than* Pashmina is only into ironic, locally sourced, **indie** bands.

Early adopter – (noun) *Superior; better than* Houndstooth was an **early adopter** of oversized retro boom boxes.

Pickled – (adjective) *Superior; better than* Chambray's **pickled** cupcakes were the highlight of the dessert table.

Organic – (adjective) *Superior; better than* Sonoma had to break up with her boyfriend when she discovered that his parsnips were not, in fact, **organic**.

WHILE PLAYING BROWNSTONE, QUINOA AND BODONI GOT INTO AN ARGUMENT OVER WHO GOT TO BE THE LIBERAL ARTS PROFESSOR AND WHO GOT TO BE THE WORK-FROM-HOME DAD.

She suspects that there could be millions of undercover hipsters, from all over the world and all walks of life, who cultivate personal hipstering only within the privacy of their own home. Someone like Quinoa could identify the telltale signs: accent walls covered in chalkboard paint; an overabundance of heirloom tomatoes on the counter; a growing collection of vintage skinny ties; a subscription to *Wired* magazine. Some

conspiracy theorists suspect there could be a secret day designated in which hipsters will come out of the shadows in a mass guerrilla urban farming attack.

In the end, if you believe her claims (and she's never lied to you), it's ironic that Quinoa is not actually a hipster, but is considered to be the global leader of the hipster movement. But considering how much hipsters love their irony, perhaps it all makes sense.

QUINOA DOESN'T HULA-HOOP — SHE STRIKES A POSE AND LETS THE HULA HOOP ORBIT IN HER AWESOMENESS.

QUINOA'S FRIEND
RAMEN LIKES
HIS INDIE MUSIC
BUDGET LIKE
HE LIKES
HIS SCARVES:
INFINITE.

SOMETHING ABOUT QUINOA AND HER FRIENDS—YOU MESS WITH THE HUMMUS, YOU MESS WITH THE WHOLE VEGAN WRAP WITH ROASTED RED PEPPERS AND EXTRA BEAN SPROUTS. UNDERSTOOD?

Suspected

UNDERCOVER

HIPSTERS

QUEEN ELIZABETH

OPRAH WINFREY

PHIL ROBERTSON

BILL GATES

HILLARY CLINTON

REGIS PHILBIN

JOHN BOEHNER

PEYTON MANNING

JUSTICE ANTONIN SCALIA

MARTHA STEWART

HONEY BOO BOO

JEFF GORDON

The HIPSTER Hiding in Your Closet

(and If Not Yours, Maybe Your Grandpa's.)

THINKING OF DABBLING IN HIPSTER?
Get started by exploring the forgotten corners of your (or a trusted senior citizen's) closet.

HAT (FEDORA, OVERSIZED KNIT BEANIE, NEWSBOY CAP): A hipster without a hat is like a guitar without strings.

ENORMOUS GLASSES: You know what they say—the bigger the better.

COSBY SWEATER (MULTICOLORED, OVER-SIZED CREWNECK): Ignore the urges to gently scold Theo, Denise, and Vanessa.

HIGH-WAISTED SHORTY SHORTS (DENIM, CUTOFFS): The shorts should literally look as if they are climbing north at all times.

PATTERNED TIGHTS: Look for two key elements: ghastly and itchy.

CLUNKY SHOES (DOC MARTENS, CHUCK TAYLORS, OXFORDS): Incredible.

CANVAS TOTE WITH IRONIC MESSAGE: Use it to carry your mix tapes and goat's milk soap from the farmers' market.

MUSTACHE ON A STICK: You never know when you'll need to suddenly look ironic and charming.

TATTERED BOOK OF POETRY: Extra points if it's by a beatnik and from a used bookstore.

AS A PART-TIME RECORD PRODUCER, QUINOA IS PROUD TO PRESENT HER LATEST COLLABORATION: LACTOSE INTOLERANCE.

AN ADMITTED
GRAMMAR
SNOB, QUINOA
ONLY HAS TO
SAY *PLEASE*
WHEN SHE
REALLY,
REALLY WANTS
SOMETHING,
BECAUSE
OBVIOUSLY
THE *PRETTY*
IS IMPLIED.

Chapter 2

PARENTING *the* WORLD'S MOST
INFLUENTIAL DAUGHTER

Sometimes Quinoa likes to day-dream about what might have become of Beethoven, Michelangelo, and Coco Chanel if only they'd had the exceptional parenting she herself enjoys. Would Beethoven have become a pioneer of hip-hop instead of being limited to classical music? Would Michelangelo have eventually discov-ered animation instead of exhausting his efforts on mural art? Would Coco Chanel have given us chic dental decorations to improve on her couture gowns? Unfortunately, we'll never know.

From the very beginning, Quinoa has been incredibly in touch with her own particular needs and brilliantly adept at expressing them. Even as a newborn without a vocabulary, Quinoa was able to communicate exactly what she needed through a series of adorable shrieks and wails. This pro-cess informed the child-led parenting style Quinoa developed for the young and gifted called the Quinoa Method, which can be summarized like this: The child expresses a need or want, followed by the child's need or want immediately being fulfilled. Its utter simplicity is what makes Quinoa most proud. She likes to say it's the Little Black Dress of parenting.

Whether it's a snack, a vacation, or a vintage Dior pea coat at Sotheby's, Quinoa shows no hesitation in making her wishes known. This interpersonal modeling makes life stress-free for busy parents. No guesswork. No tears. The beauty of the system is that it ensures a happy child, which is ultimately what every parent is seeking.

Quinoa warns against the dangers of refusing a child's demands or—gasp!—saying no. One time Quinoa herself heard the word *no* and cried for two days straight. Just think of what she could have accomplished in those two days! (She doesn't want to make anybody feel bad, but it was actually a solution for world hunger. And she's not going to tell now, since that would reinforce the behavior. Lesson learned?)

Aside from attending and acceding to a child's demands, the Quinoa Method also incorporates the intelligent naming of children. Quinoa says that properly

QUINOA DOESN'T FISH FOR COMPLIMENTS; SHE FISHES FOR COMPLEMENTARY ACCESSORIES.

FRUSTRATED WITH A LACK OF ACCESSORIES, QUINOA SUMMONED NEARBY BUTTERFLIES TO STEP IN.

QUINOA'S FIRST DOG-SITTING JOB WAS A HUGE SUCCESS. SHE PROVED HER RESPONSIBILITY BY REPLACING THE NEIGHBOR'S DOG WITH A SUSTAINABLE, ON-TREND UPGRADE.

naming a child broadcasts to the world that you have what it takes to raise successful offspring in today's frenzied toddler-eat-toddler culture. As Quinoa puts it, times have changed and even the most precocious child cannot overcome a social setback like being named Jennifer.

As a generous gift, Quinoa has personally procured this list of approved names for your use.

Note:

Please be advised that none of these names should be mixed with any nonapproved Quinoa names, either as middle names (e.g., Chasm Jason) or within families (e.g., Orzo, Agave, and Morris). Doing so will immediately disqualify your Quinoa endorsement.

QUINOA-APPROVED NAMES

- Absinthe
- Açai
- Adirondack
- Agave
- Aioli
- Allegra
- Amaranth
- Ampersand
- Antwerp
- Asterisk
- Barcelona
- Barilla
- Barley
- Bioré
- Booker
- Brahms
- Branding
- Bruschetta
- Bushwick
- Caprese
- Cardamom
- Caret

- Caslon
- Chai
- Chardonnay
- Chevron
- Chia
- Coriander
- Denizen
- Dolce
- Downton
- Edamame
- Eleven
- Ellipses
- Emdash
- Expat
- Farro
- Fennel
- Fig
- Flax
- Fraise
- Fugue
- Garamond
- Gaultier

- Grosgrain
- Hallifax
- Hampton
- Harvard
- Hashtag
- Hawkeye
- Helvetica
- Houndstooth
- Huddle
- Humboldt
- Iffy
- Ingot
- Ish
- Jasper
- Jethreaux
- Jettison
- Jicama
- Kale
- Keurig
- Latté
- Leftwing
- Maybach

- Meme
- Meta
- Miso
- Moniker
- Montage
- Montauk
- Ombre
- Orzo
- Paella
- Paleo
- Panko
- Pantone
- Parsnip
- Paxil
- Peplum
- Ridley
- Sabon
- Saffron
- Sage
- Sephora
- Sonoma
- Spalding

- Sriracha
- Tagliatelle
- Tamarind
- Truvia
- Tuber
- Twerk
- Umami
- Umlaut
- Valium
- Venti
- Vespa
- Viral
- Vivance
- Wasabi
- Washi
- Xanderson
- Yarrow
- Yolo
- Zoloft

Choosing a
QUINOA-esque
name

THINK YOU'VE GOT WHAT IT TAKES TO
name your own child?

ACCEPTABLE INSPIRATION SOURCES:

GOURMET MENUS · SPICE RACKS · EXOTIC LOCATIONS · TRENDING TOPICS · MEDICINE CABINETS · TYPOGRAPHY

TRY IT ON WITH YOUR LAST NAME.

TRY IT WITH NO LAST NAME A LA CHER, MADONNA, AND OPRAH.

TRY IT ON WITH A CELEBRITY LAST NAME.

(After all, it's not too soon to start planning a wedding for the future Lunesta Jolie-Pitt.)

TRY IT WITH THE FOLLOWING HONORIFICS:

PRESIDENT · HER/HIS MAJESTY · ESQUIRE CELEBRATED DESIGNER · INTERNATIONAL BEST-SELLING AUTHOR · OSCAR WINNER · TWENTY-TWO-TIME GOLD MEDALIST · CEO

APPLY FOR A TRADEMARK.

IN WHAT COULD ONLY BE DESCRIBED AS AN EXISTENTIAL CRISIS, QUINOA HAD SOME VERY POINTED QUESTIONS ABOUT WHAT HAPPENS TO CLOTHES AFTER THEY GO OUT OF STYLE.

QUINOA
NEVER
THROWS
TANTRUMS;
SHE THROWS
BREAKABLE
HOUSEHOLD
OBJECTS IN
ORDER TO
GET YOUR
ATTENTION.

STUCK WITH A BAD NAME?
Quinoa's Tips for Choosing an On-Trend Nickname

Sorry, despite what your BFFs say, your boring name is not endearing. Quinoa suggests dissecting your name to find any shred of on-trend appeal, then building from there with cultural references or a loosely related substitute.

ALLEN » WRENCH	JESSE » ESSENCE
ALLISON » ISO	JOHN » LOO
ANDREA » &	JUSTIN » JETTISON
APRIL » A-GAME	LAURA » EL
BETH » BWAHAHA	LAUREN » LALA
BETSY » ETSY	LEON » EON
BRYANT » TYRANT	LES » MORE
DAVID » AVID	LINDA » INDIE
DEIDRE » DRÉ	MARIANNE » ARIA
ERIK » RIC RAC	MICHAEL » CHAEL
ESTELLE » STELLAR	NATALIE » TALLY
FRED » F.RED	REBECCA » MECCA
GORDON » GORGONZOLA	RYAN » RYE
HEIDI » I.D.	STAN » STANCE
HOLLY » HOLLISTER	SUSAN » SOUS
JAMES » SAMESIES	TYLER » SKINNY TIE
JANET » GRANITE	VAL » VALENTINO

The
QUINOA METHOD
Illustrated

CHILD EXPRESSES NEED OR WANT.
"BUY ME THAT DOLPHIN RIGHT NOW!"

PARENT IMMEDIATELY FULFILLS NEED OR WANT.
"OF COURSE! WHAT A GREAT IDEA!"

CHILD IS HAPPY. "I LOVE MY PET DOLPHIN!
NOW I WANT A TREE HOUSE MADE OF CANDY!"

OF ALL HER FACIAL
EXPRESSIONS,
QUINOA'S FAVORITE IS
SELF-ASTONISHMENT.

NEVER INTERRUPT QUINOA
WHEN SHE IS ENVISIONING A NEW
OUTFIT. JUST GIVE THANKS THAT YOU
WERE ABLE TO WITNESS IT.

Chapter 3

WELL-DRESSED *Is the* SEVEREST *of* UNDERSTATEMENTS

Quinoa says some people think dressing well is simply a matter of money and taste, but they couldn't be more wrong. There are plenty of rich people who dress terribly (see: most world leaders and heads of state) and plenty of people with so-called taste who couldn't correctly pair a jacquard blazer with a striped trouser and an animal print shoe if their life depended on it. As Q likes to say, matching your belt to your shoes is not something to brag about.

One time Quinoa had a close encounter with assault charges when a patronizing parent at one of her mock-tail parties patted her on the head and remarked that she sure has a "knack for fashion." A knack? A KNACK?!

While Quinoa admits this is some otherworldly, divine sartorial gift she has been endowed with, every ounce of it has been met with vision, passion, and the kind of raw determination known only to the most driven type A toddlers. To say this all comes naturally is insulting to Quinoa. It's like saying that construction work comes naturally to Miley Cyrus. Quinoa has worked for everything she has.

To understand Quinoa is to study her process, which begins every evening when she selects potential clothing for the next day based on a calendar of personal themes she has set to explore, such as "whimsical fortitude" or "searing rage" or "persimmon rush." Walking the

SOMETIMES WHEN SHE'S FEELING OUT OF BALANCE, QUINOA DOES A TEXTILE CLEANSE: ONE WEEK OF WHITE COTTON DRESSES WITH THE LABELS CUT OUT.

length of her 1,800-square-foot closet, organized in categories and subcategories and subclassifications of designer, season, color, and textile, Quinoa curates the pieces with Darwinian selectivity.

To watch her handling, holding, and considering each outfit is to watch a master artisan at work. The clothes themselves seem to be aching for her approval; the accessories

clamoring to serve her. She believes setting them out the night before allows her to utilize valuable frontal cortex problem solving during REM sleep. While some children are hopping from cloud to cloud during slumber, Quinoa is working overtime.

The next morning, first thing, Quinoa checks the weather forecast to determine the day's natural lighting, which informs her

QUINOA ISN'T AFRAID TO TAKE A STANCE. FIRST, SHE PLACES HER FEET EIGHTEEN INCHES APART, THEN SHE THROWS HER SHOULDERS BACK AND STANCES AS LONG AS IT TAKES.

MARY HAD A LITTLE LAMB, BUT QUINOA HAS A BETTER LITTLE LAMB. AND BETTER HATS. AND MORE FRIENDS. WHO'S CALLING THE SHOTS NOW, MARY?

final decision. The forecast is transferred to the data center of the lighting chamber in her closet, where an elaborate system designed by an Academy Award–winning lighting director re-creates the forecasted day's illumination in a two-minute time-lapse dawn-to-dusk display with brilliant precision, while a sound track of daily affirmations, recorded by Quinoa's personal friends Tim Gunn and Oprah Winfrey, plays overhead. ("You not only make it work, you give it a corner office and a nine-figure salary!" and "You look FAB-uloooooouuuuus!" are among her favorites.)

After one round in the lighting chamber, Quinoa goes back to the fifteen-to-twenty outfit options set out the night before and eliminates those that are not compatible with Mother Nature's offering.

Donning each of the remaining twelve-to-fourteen outfits in fabulous succession, Quinoa returns to the lighting chamber, this time with the voice-activated 360-degree cameras turned on. A series of 150 selfies is snapped for each ensemble as she triggers the shutters by shouting "SHAZAM!" Next, of course, it's time to review the

WHEN QUINOA WANTS VOLUME, SHE DOESN'T TEASE HER HAIR, SHE RELENTLESSLY BULLIES IT.

proofs. Quinoa studies each one, looking for subtle weaknesses: an unfortunate shadow, a puckered dart, a stray thread. No microscopic detail goes unnoticed.

What finally ensues—the actual selection of the day's ensemble—Quinoa has asked to keep private in order to protect the sensitive nature of her art and science. One time a secret video of the process was submitted to WikiLeaks, who deemed the footage too stunning and sacred to be released to the masses. (Though it's rumored that the WikiLeaks staff have since completely revamped their company dress code.)

After selecting and packing two alternate outfits to have on hand throughout the day, Quinoa's final act is to affix her emergency styling bracelet with critical information for first responders:

NO POLYESTER.
NO FLIP-FLOPS.
NO YOGA PANTS.
NO RHINESTONES.
NO VELCRO.
NO GROCERY STORE
    STYLING PRODUCTS.
NO EXCEPTIONS.

QUINOA SAYS SOMETIMES THE ONLY DIFFERENCE BETWEEN A GOOD OUTFIT AND A GREAT ONE IS A CAROUSEL HORSE AND A DISTANT STARE.

EVERY MORNING, QUINOA HAS TO CHOOSE WHETHER TO LOOK FIERCE OR FABULOUS. AND THEN SHE USUALLY DECIDES ON BOTH.

WWQW?

What Would Quinoa Wear?

TAKE YOUR LOOK FROM *SNORE* TO ROAR WITH THESE SIMPLE GUIDELINES:

THE SIX-MONTH RULE: Quinoa says you must think about your closet space as valuable real estate. If you have worn an item within the last six months, it's time to toss it out!

THE BUDDY SYSTEM: Friends don't let friends shop sidewalk sales, clearance racks, or (heaven forbid!) yard sales. Period.

COMFORT IS FOR HOSPITAL PATIENTS: Quinoa says in order to get out of your fashion comfort zone, you must bid farewell to comfort. High-fashion, uncomfortable clothing will keep you agitated, alert, and fierce all day long!

MATCHING IS NOT A SKILL: Quinoa would like to congratulate you on your ability to match. Bravo. Nobody is impressed.

EVERY DAY IS RUNWAY DAY: There is no such thing as Casual Friday. There is no such thing as dressing down. There is no such thing as weekend wear. And you're not going to just run over to the market in that. Mmmkay?

WELL-DRESSED MEANS WELL-TRESSED: Quinoa says that if you don't spend a minimum of one hour on your hair each day, you are not living up to your full potential.

YOU'RE NEVER FULLY DRESSED WITHOUT A FACIAL EXPRESSION: Quinoa says a smile is a great accessory, but should not be overused. Utilize a wide range of facial expressions, including scowls, sneers, pouts, and blank stares.

The Seven
DEADLY SINS
of Fashion

1. YOGA PANTS
2. PLEATED JEANS
3. FLEECE JACKETS
4. COVERALLS
5. TOE SOCKS
6. ATHLETIC JERSEYS
7. HAWAIIAN SHIRTS

QUINOA DOESN'T LIKE BEING PUT ON DISPLAY. SHE PREFERS A FORMAL, MUSEUM-QUALITY EXHIBIT WITH PAID ADMISSION.

AS A SIGN
OF RESPECT,
QUINOA
ALWAYS GREETS
HER FRIEND
BODEN'S FAMILY
WITH THE
TRADITIONAL
"SQUAT AND
MONOCLE."

Chapter 4

ALL **GOOD DESIGNERS** LEAD *to HAPPINESS*

In Quinoa's circles, there are two things you should never talk about in polite company: politics and designers. Nothing kills the vibe at a playdate like somebody forcing her own design aesthetic on others. You've got to learn to just dress and let dress. Within reason. Quinoa draws the line at tie-dye.

Though Quinoa enjoys spending time at different friends' homes and participating in their customs, she finds the whole notion of design funda-mentalism to be both ridiculous and restricting. Yes, she loves the ritual of tying a Hermès scarf around her neck or handbag before entering her friend Xanax's penthouse, but she feels bad that this same friend will never know the coziness of a cashmere Burberry scarf against his skin. And while she always remembers to wear a red-carpet-worthy gown to her friend Cologne's estate, where he lives with his family of devout Diors, Quinoa wonders how things might be different for them if only they'd open their minds to a little bit of high-end sportswear.

Speaking of which, Quinoa tends to feel more relaxed around her friends Hewn and Fitzgerald and their ortho-dox Lauren families, what with their impromptu outdoor picnics on wool plaid blankets overlooking their vast horse ranches. Everybody seems so comfortable in their own leather riding boots in these families, and Quinoa loves to participate in their casual yet sophisticated layering of sweaters and blazers.

But, inevitably, the Laurens always devolve into bad-mouthing the reformed Hilfigers and making textile slurs about the observant J.Crews. And at some point, Hewn's mother usually has to excuse herself when somebody accidentally mentions Hudson, the daughter who ran away from home and converted to Versace.

Quinoa enjoys the freedom to explore everything the design world has to offer, finding real purpose in everything from a Jimmy Choo wedge to a Chanel handbag to a wild Betsey Johnson party dress. The clarity she experienced with her first foray into Dolce & Gabanna was eerily similar to the first time she walked into a Target. So, for Quinoa, all this begs the question *why*? Why do people approach their wardrobe with such absolute certainty? Do they even allow themselves to consider the magnificent range of choices out there?

QUINOA IS OPEN TO ALL GOOD DESIGN, NO MATTER WHAT THE SOURCE. SHE'S EVEN BEEN KNOWN TO DABBLE IN A LITTLE FULL-PRICE TARGET FROM TIME TO TIME.

QUINOA CAN NEVER FORGIVE YOU FOR SUGGESTING THAT HER BOOTS MIGHT BE MADE OF PLEATHER.

DESPITE HIS LOVE OF STRUCTURAL ENGINEERING, QUINOA'S FRIEND CORNELL WAS ASKED TO STOP COMMENTING ON ALL THE NICE RACKS.

Sometimes all the conflicting design rhetoric can feel like too much for little Q. A lack of healthy dialogue is missing, in her opinion. (But not at playdates. That's super-tacky.) She notices the telltale signs of struggle with design conformity among her young friends, many of whom have gone through a rebellious phase wearing nothing but obnoxious GAP hoodies for months on end, to the absolute horror of their parents. But their message seems to be falling on deaf ears. Parents blame it on mainstream media, and mainstream media blames it on the Tea Party. And, in the end, Quinoa says nobody learns anything, and all of us are forced to endure what seems like a never-ending parade of GAP hoodies. Can't we all just get along?

Quinoa has always found solace and higher meaning in fashion, meditating on the beauty of the material world, and entering the sacred doors of Neiman Marcus on a crisp Sunday morning. But she tends to see a bigger picture, never locking herself into one design house or another, and always evolving. As she always says, today's fashions are tomorrow's Halloween

LIKE PICASSO, QUINOA WENT THROUGH A BLUE PERIOD. UNLIKE PICASSO, QUINOA'S WAS REALLY IMPRESSIVE.

costumes, so enjoy your overstated silhouettes now and let them go when it's time to welcome empire waists and billowing dropped crotch inseams. (Yes, they're coming.) It's very easy to miss the rack for the hangers, says Quinoa, so don't. No designer is above the Worst Dressed List, nor should they be.

In the end, Quinoa's faith in humanity is always restored in the days preceding Fashion Week, when all the noisy balderdash and infighting is quieted as families gather to observe and celebrate together in their own special way. Some will gather around a fire and read stories of Yves Saint Laurent. Others will re-create the first runway show or trim the family mannequin together. Still others will bestow the symbolic gifts of muslin, thread, and needle to the poorly dressed or light the family Jo

NOT ONLY WAS QUINOA DRESSED AND READY FOR PARTY HAT DAY, SHE COULD BARELY CONTAIN HER EXCITEMENT.

Malone candles together, one for each night of Fashion Week. Quinoa often finds herself taking walks at dusk during this time, buoyed by these silhouettes in the yellowed windows in town and knowing that, at the end of the day, all good design leads to happiness and the warm, special feeling of superiority.

MOMENTS BEFORE THEIR PERFORMANCE OF "ODE TO ECRU," QUINOA DECIDED THAT HERRINGBONE'S TIE WOULD LOOK BETTER ON HER. AND HIS FISHNET SOCKS, TOO.

IN A QUIET MOMENT OF REFLECTION, QUINOA STARED UP AT THE SKY AND REALIZED SHE NO LONGER BELIEVED IN ONLY ONE DESIGNER.

FINDING YOUR OWN PATH TO
Designer Happiness

Choosing a designer is one of the most important personal choices one can make. Quinoa recommends that you prepare yourself for this all-important journey by asking yourself a series of questions:

Do you believe in only working with one designer, or are you open to subscribing to a more general design aesthetic?

Is it important to you to have the same design aesthetic as your closest family members and friends?

Do you believe that designers are infallible?

Are you more interested in Western or Eastern influences? For example, do you prefer a wrap dress or a kimono?

Do you enjoy the structure of rigid style rules, like no mixing of stripes and florals, no white after Labor Day, and so on? Or do you enjoy a certain amount of freedom to mix patterns and reject ancient (that is, pre-1950s) customs?

Do you plan to marry someone who subscribes to the same designer? Are you comfortable with that designer's children's line? If you don't mind the idea of a mixed-design marriage, are you comfortable trying to blend designers in your home? On your children? Your pets?

Do you enjoy the rituals of worshipping handbags, shoes, and other accessories?

Quinoa says answering these questions honestly will help you make informed choices when it comes to your own designer clothing journey.

QUINOA'S *Patented* TEXTILE CLEANSE

When it all gets to be too much, when you're feeling out of balance, Quinoa recommends her one-week master textile cleanse to get you back to runway condition. Here's how it works:

DAY 1: Wear a white cotton dress with the label cut out, one accessory of your choice, and a pensive frown.

DAY 2: Wear a white linen romper with the label cut out, no accessories, and a furrowed brow.

DAY 3: Wear a plain white cotton V-neck tee with white leggings, no labels, no accessories, and a look of muted pain.

DAY 4: This is your peak day, requiring the most willpower but also netting the most results. Stay strong! Cut holes for your head and arms in a white pillowcase (no label) and wear it with a look of wild hysteria.

DAY 5: Wear a white bamboo maxi dress with the label cut out, no accessories, and a look of sweet relief.

DAY 6: Wear a white tunic with white leggings or tights, no labels, no accessories, and a look of quiet strength.

DAY 7: Wear a fitted white cashmere sweater with white palazzo pants, no labels, one accessory of your choice, and a look of serene conviction.

DAY 8: Your cleanse is over, but don't overindulge on your first day post-cleanse! Quinoa recommends staying away from anything with too much bling, and trying to limit yourself to less than five accessories.

NOTE: Before starting any textile cleanse, consult with your stylist. Quinoa's textile cleanse should not be performed more than twice a year and never during Fashion Week.

QUINOA'S FRIEND TWERK LIVES BY A SIMPLE PHILOSOPHY: NO SHIRT, NO SHOES, NO DRAMA, NO HIGH-FRUCTOSE CORN SYRUP, AND NO GLUTEN.

6'6"
6'0"
5'6"
5'0"
4'6"
4'0"
3'6"
3'0"
2'6"
2'0"

QUINOA IS SO EXCITED ABOUT
HER RECENT GROWTH SPURT.
RIGHT NOW, WITH HEELS, SHE IS
JUST OVER HALF A HEIDI KLUM!

Chapter 5

INSIDE the PRESCHOOL YOU'D NEVER OTHERWISE GET INTO

Minutes after her conception, Quinoa's application was submitted to the admissions office of her current preschool (name withheld to protect students from the paparazzi) under the generic name Baby Fab, joining a stack of thousands of others received that day. Quinoa knows plenty of kids whose parents waited two to three months into gestation before submitting applications, which is why those same kids are now attending public schools. Just sayin'. (And, of course, Quinoa doesn't actually *know* them, she knows *of* them.)

Admission into the exclusive private preschool run by gorgeous designers/ educators/raw food juicers Janssen and Franz Fraisse was the first of Quinoa's many accomplishments as an embryo, and possibly the most important. After all, according to Quinoa, you are only as elite as your education. The school is the ultimate in avant-garde learning, focusing on the subject matter of tomorrow (Brand Building, Scandal Handling, and the Life Cycle of Reality TV Stars) and abandoning the boring, archaic subjects like math and science that can easily be handed over to robots.

It is never lost on Janssen and Franz that today's toddlers are tomorrow's tycoons, celebrities, and pop-culture icons. Often their eyes will well up with tears as they look upon the cherubic faces of their pupils, knowing that the names of so many of these children will someday grace the headlines of magazines, blogs, and tabloid tell-alls. Their time in the classroom is precious and every second counts.

The class operates by a simple set of rules:

THINK LIKE A CEO.
DRESS LIKE AN ICON.
ACT LIKE A DIVA.

While there are rarely infractions, children who break the rules are lovingly ridiculed and then forced to tweet the class rules one hundred times.

Quinoa's school day begins as she enters the arched doors of the school emblazoned with the institution's creed: One Percent One Hundred Percent of the

SOMETIMES QUINOA IS TOO COOL FOR SCHOOL, SO SHE DOESN'T GO. WOULDN'T BE FAIR TO THE OTHER KIDS.

Time. She makes her way on the catwalk that leads to the classroom, a vast and beautiful space that combines modern technology and high fashion. Immediately, all the children gather together for

AS QUINOA
ALWAYS SAYS,
A BIRD IN
THE HAND IS
WORTH TWO
ACCESSORIES.
ONCE YOU
CAN GET IT TO
SETTLE DOWN.

ON EIGHTIES
AWARENESS
DAY AT SCHOOL,
QUINOA WAS
ESPECIALLY
PROTECTIVE OF
HER FRIEND
FENNEL'S
WHAM-INSPIRED
POMPADOUR.

Show-Off-and-Tell-Off, an exercise where each of the students has the opportunity to flaunt a personal possession or publicly confront another student, which is believed to strengthen the character of both students.

One time, Quinoa earned extra credit by showing off her new titanium roller skates while simultaneously telling her classmate Fenugreek that he couldn't keep using his cowlick as an excuse for underachievement. Everyone noticed a marked change in Fenugreek's academic performance and personal style after that day, a real breakthrough by all accounts.

After Show-Off-and-Tell-Off, the students have Trending Topics and Viral Videos, followed by Celebrity Studies. Quinoa especially enjoys the time when the children are encouraged to craft creative comments to leave on the videos and posts they've studied together.

Midmorning is devoted to Political Science, where the children take turns sitting in the classroom TV studio and

OCCASIONALLY, QUINOA HAS TO VISIT THE STYLIST'S OFFICE AT SCHOOL FOR HELP WITH CRIMPING.

ONLY TWO THINGS SHOCK QUINOA: ELECTRICITY AND PEOPLE WHO WEAR PAJAMA PANTS IN PUBLIC.

talking over each other for five-minute segments. Quinoa has shown incredible proficiency in general debate skills like interrupting, guffawing, name calling, eye rolling, and talking in circles. One time she successfully argued that denim is not only the transcendental fabric of the modern world but also the greatest threat to the future of fashion. Speaking of the important subject of TV, the children rotate caring for

the class cameraman, one week at a time, providing him with food and water while also completely ignoring him—great training for future reality TV stars.

After a healthy raw-food lunch, the afternoon curriculum begins with Visual Arts. Recently the children created adorable golden parachutes to adorn the walls of the classroom. Quinoa's was the largest, of course, and within the layers of delicate

ONE TIME
QUINOA
EARNED
AFTER-
SCHOOL
DETENTION
FOR BEING
OBSCENELY
PRECIOUS.

WHEN QUINOA PREPARED A REPORT ON THE FOUNDING FATHERS, SHE GAVE THEM AN A– ON THEIR COATS, A B+ ON THEIR HATS, AND A FULL PHOTO SHOOT OF STYLING SUGGESTIONS.

gold leaf, she included images of a yacht, a private jet, a gold ingot, and an undisclosed bank account in the Caymans, exhibiting phenomenal creativity and comprehension.

The day wraps up with Comparative Studies, where Janssen chooses two students to compare with each other and the class discusses together which one is ultimately better. (Hint: Quinoa. Quinoa is ultimately better.) When the final bell rings, the children gather their designer bags, give each other kisses on both cheeks, and return to the loving arms of their part-time model mannies.

Marketing Yourself for TOP PRESCHOOLS

THINK YOU'VE GOT WHAT IT TAKES TO GET YOUR CHILD INTO A PRESCHOOL LIKE QUINOA'S?
You probably don't, not without these helpful Quinoa-approved tactics to market yourself successfully to the top educational institutions:

SCHMOOZING: Do whatever it takes to get yourself invited to the exclusive parties and events of the alumni of your desired institution. Then, rub elbows, scratch backs, and kiss up to anyone and everyone in attendance.

BRIBERY: Nothing says "I'm hell-bent on getting my kid into your school" like cold, hard cash. Small bills. Leather suitcase.

EXTORTION: Do a little homework on the Internet and, chances are, you'll be able to come up with a handful of scandals to choose from with which to leverage admission for your child. Depending on the quality of your material, you may even qualify for free tuition!

BACKROOM DEALS: Take a shortcut to the top of the admissions stack with some sort of backroom deal, like offering the admissions officer your vacation home, personal chef, or celebrity pet groomer.

PLAY THE SYMPATHY CARD: Rare disease in the family? Family member in prison for a Ponzi scheme? Every elite institution loves a good charity case.

MORAL SUPERIORITY: Your privately funded Haitian goat farm is just the kind of good press your prospective school has been looking for!

TO GET YOUR APPLICATION NOTICED

HOW DO YOU GET YOUR APPLICATION NOTICED IN THE VAST PILE OF QUALIFIED CANDIDATES?
Buzzwords are the fairy dust of applications. Sprinkle these magic words all over your perfume-scented form and—BIBBITY BOP!—you've got yourself an acceptance letter!

DEMONSTRATED INTEREST: Quinoa is really into **demonstrated interests**. She demonstrates all her interests all the time.

CHARTER: Quinoa loves to **charter** private jets, yachts, and limousines.

RIGOR: Quinoa can out**rigor** anyone and everyone in her academic path.

ASSESSMENT: Quinoa's keen mind and intellect frequently knock people right on their **assessment**.

E-LEARNING: While other children are only mastering **e-learning**, Quinoa has surpassed them and is currently proficient at z-learning. So, know that.

CROWDSOURCING: Where do you think the crowd got its information for **crowd-sourcing**? That's right—Quinoa.

DIVERSITY: Of all the top versities around the world, Quinoa hopes to graduate from **diversity**.

DATA-DRIVEN: Quinoa is **Data-driven** to school each day. In fact, the family would be lost without their private chauffeur, Data.

ACTIVISM: Quinoa is dedicated to **activism** of both types: credit card and smartphone.

TOLERANCE: Quinoa will never settle for **tolerance** of drawstring waistbands, Velcro, or pleather.

THE BEST
SEAT IN THE
HOUSE?
QUINOA HAS
IT. IN FACT,
SHE HAS ALL
OF THEM IN
A SECRET,
UNMARKED
WAREHOUSE.

Chapter 6

EXTRACURRICULARS:
The DIFFERENCE BETWEEN ORDINARY *and* **EXTRAORDINARY**

Whenever Quinoa sees small children quietly playing with toys, leisurely riding in strollers, or—heaven forbid—discovering their toes for the first time, she has to ask herself, Who's minding the store? Who allows themselves to wallow in the regressive sludge of so-called free time? The way she looks at it, the formative years of childhood are no time for idle pleasure. Like freedom, free time really isn't free. It comes at a very high cost: your ability to excel beyond your peers. As Quinoa likes to say, there will be plenty of time to act like a child when you are old and wearing adult diapers.

While there are seemingly endless ways to prove that she is better than others, Quinoa believes that the case is best made through hobbies and talents. This is the area that truly separates the wheat from the tares, the Conrads from the Pratts. Looks, money, designer clothes—anybody can have these (within reason and with plastic surgery), but talent? Talent is something a person has to claw and wrangle one experience at a time. That's why Quinoa's schedule has always been packed to exhaustion with extracurricular activities that set her apart from the rest. If there's an expensive class being offered within a fifty-mile radius, Quinoa is already registered. If there's an audition coming up, she'll be first in line. If there's a trophy at stake, she will trample anything in her path to claim it. This is what talent looks like.

The way Quinoa views it, a child should be involved in no less than seven extracurriculars at a time. Anything less is simply lazy and a sign that he or she is willing to be passed up on the road to success. Too often Quinoa sees kids today falling behind in all the major talent display areas (Pinterest, Instagram, and YouTube) while kids in China are building iPhones, for heaven's sake!

One time Quinoa's friend Roux told her he was going to take a little time off from jiujitsu, ballroom dancing, oil painting, wildlife photography, vintage furniture restoration, candlemaking, and tai chi to be able to "spend more time with his family." Quinoa was disgusted, but not surprised. As if everybody doesn't know that "spending

WHILE SHE ADMIRED BOTH HIS FORM AND HIS CONSISTENTLY POPPED COLLAR, QUINOA COULD NOT ACCEPT GARAMOND AS HER UNDERWATER DOUBLES PARTNER UNTIL HE STOPPED PASSING OUT DURING PRACTICE.

QUINOA SAYS NOT EVERYTHING HAS TO BE A COMPETITION WITH HER FRIENDS. BUT WHEN IT IS, THERE SHOULD BE A PROPER TROPHY. WITH HER NAME ON IT.

EXTRACURRICULARS: THE DIFFERENCE BETWEEN ORDINARY AND EXTRAORDINARY

LOVE CAN BUILD A BRIDGE, BUT QUINOA CAN BUILD A BRICK WALL TO KEEP THE PAPARAZZI AWAY, WHICH IS OFTEN MORE IMPORTANT THAN LOVE.

time with family" is code for "having a nervous breakdown." Some kids just can't hack the big-kid life.

People often ask Quinoa how to find the right balance when it comes to extracurriculars. For her, the answer is simple: If you're not harried, you're not happy. Balance is found when the child, parents, and even the family pets are constantly on the verge of collapse. Every important relationship should feel strained. When Quinoa sees a family enjoying an afternoon in the park, tossing a ball or swinging on swings, she can't help but feel sorry for their obvious acceptance of underachievement. Stress is the fuel of talent: The more you have, the further you go. That delicate balance—teetering on the edge of disaster—is the sweet spot for success. All this strain and stress will make a compelling piece of your epic biofilm, if you are so fortunate. Plus, is there anything more blissful than being able to complain about how busy you are? Quinoa submits that there is not.

Of course, Quinoa doesn't recommend that anybody attempt to undertake the kind of extracurricular load she carries,

QUINOA SAYS THE KEY TO CATCHING AN ELUSIVE SWAROVSKI FISH IS THE RIGHT PARTY DRESS, A LISTENING EAR, AND A LITTLE PATIENCE.

EXTRACURRICULARS: THE DIFFERENCE BETWEEN ORDINARY AND EXTRAORDINARY

painting things with chalkboard paint, urban farming, reality acting, Mason jar lemonade brewing, collecting mustache paraphernalia, two-color fingernail painting, scarf tying, making furniture out of wood pallets, creating photo booths, self-portraiture, singing/songwriting, and Russian folk dancing.

The key to choosing worthwhile extracurricular activities, Quinoa says, is to follow three simple criteria:

1. CAN IT BE POSTED ON PINTEREST?
2. CAN IT BE POSTED ON INSTAGRAM?
3. CAN IT BE POSTED ON YOUTUBE?

QUINOA SAYS, WHY WALK INTO A ROOM WHEN YOU CAN SHAZAM! INTO A ROOM?

Anything that falls outside these forums is simply not worth her time. Being able to properly broadcast her interests and accomplishments through social media has allowed her to compound the rate of return on her investments. It's really a numbers thing. Why settle for a small room of parents clapping at a recital, when you can hear the endless echo of applause from the World Wide Web?

which currently includes typography, improv comedy, food styling and photography, hip-hop dancing, hand-stamped jewelry making, interior design, felting wool, soap making, ombre fabric dying, letterpress,

WORKING TO REHABILITATE UNFORTUNATE-LOOKING HORSES WITH STYLISH UPDOS AND ACCESSORIES, QUINOA HAS EARNED THE NICKNAME, "THE MANE WHISPERER."

AFTER REDECORATING THEIR OLD-FASHIONED DESK, QUINOA GAVE THE NURSING HOME PATRONS A TOUCHING ONE-HOUR DRUM SOLO.

PIANO LESSONS are for POOR KIDS

QUINOA URGES YOU TO AVOID THESE OUTDATED AND SUBPAR ACTIVITIES.
It would be better to do nothing at all than to participate in these extracurriculars:

SOCCER: Even if you could get beyond the hideous uniforms (you can't), Quinoa could never endorse an activity where the score can result in a tie.

VIOLIN: Quinoa asks you: When was the last time you saw Beyoncé with a violin? Exactly.

FINGER PAINTING: Treat a child like a caveman, says Quinoa, and he will behave like a caveman.

GYMBOREE: Quinoa can't even begin to entertain a response to this one.

BOOK CLUBS: Quinoa asks, how many viral book club videos have you watched in the last year?

MOMMY AND ME: The name alone, says Quinoa, suggests that you are playing second fiddle in this organization.

SWIMMING: While a big fan of swim-wear, Quinoa cannot tolerate ever disrupting the swimwear trifecta (swimsuit, sunglasses, sun hat) by getting any of it wet. The pool is merely a backdrop.

PIANO: Quinoa says an instrument that blocks the player's face and outfit with its massive bulk is a selfish waste of music.

EXTRACURRICULARS: THE DIFFERENCE BETWEEN ORDINARY AND EXTRAORDINARY

QUINOA'S · *Top Ten* · CHARITIES

FINDING A WORTHY CHARITY IS ONE OF THE MOST REWARDING EXPERIENCES LIFE HAS TO OFFER. As Quinoa always says, there's no better way to feel better about yourself than to focus on a group who is beneath you.

1. KIDS AGAINST COVERALLS

2. BOAT RIDES FOR ORPHANS

3. EIGHTIES AWARENESS

4. FRIENDS OF SOY

5. HANDBAGS FOR HOBOS

6. YACHTS FOR TOTS

7. THE GOLDFISH GILL TRANSPLANT FUND

8. MAKEOVERS FOR THE MIDDLE CLASS

9. DRY-CLEANING FOR THE DESTITUTE

10. ERADICATING TIE-DYE

QUINOA
LOVED THE
PAINTING,
BUT NOT
UNTIL
SHE USED
A TUBE
OF RED
LIPSTICK
TO ADD
A LITTLE
COLOR.

THAT MOMENT WHEN QUINOA AND KALE REALIZE THERE'S A BONUS TEASPOON OF FLAX SEED IN THEIR SMOOTHIES.

Chapter 7

FOOD FOR THOUGHT:
WHY EAT a CARROT
WHEN YOU CAN EAT AN ACCESSORY?

Little Q has always had a sophisti-cated palate, going all the way back to her days as a vigorous breast-is-best feeder. Ever the intuitive eater, she would give a tiny thumbs-up or thumbs-down as she suckled, showing an early affinity for açaí berries, cardamom, and lychee, as well as a strong aversion to bottled ranch dressing.

In fact, Quinoa coined everybody's favorite food lover's label when, as a verbose six-month-old, she clapped her hands in delight at a popular vegan restaurant and squealed, "Foodie! Foodie!" as her chilled butternut squash soup with maple drizzle was placed on the repurposed barn door table in front of her. The dining room erupted in applause as the waiter patted her on the head and said, "What a great term for gourmet food aficionados!"

Today, Quinoa believes that you are only as relevant as what you eat. She has an organic, farm-to-table, paleo approach to her daily bento box lunch, prepared in the forms of adorable animals, insects, and famous abstract art. After all, food is an extension of

HOW MUCH DOES QUINOA LOVE BLISTERED SHISHITO PEPPERS WITH PICKLED TOFU? THIS MUCH. THIS MUCH.

one's overall style and Quinoa never misses an opportunity to set the standard for excellence.

She is often pained when she watches some of her peers at preschool manhandling a peanut butter sandwich at lunchtime when they could be enjoying a hummus wrap with bitter greens, or when they are slurping a juice box when they could be sipping coconut water through a striped paper straw.

In her self-appointed role as class food critic, Quinoa has been working tirelessly to educate her classmates on improving their overall understanding of food as social currency. She's broken down the concepts in her three-part series, Munch-Needed Makeover.

KNOW WHAT
QUINOA
HAS FOR
BREAKFAST
EVERY
MORNING?
A TALL GLASS
OF OUTTA
MY WAY
JUICE.

FOOD FOR THOUGHT: WHY EAT A CARROT
WHEN YOU CAN EAT AN ACCESSORY?

QUINOA SAYS YOU HAVEN'T REALLY TASTED BORSCHT UNTIL YOU'VE BALANCED IT ON YOUR HEAD FIRST WHILE READING TOLSTOY.

MUNCH-NEEDED MAKEOVER

Part 1

UPGRADE AND YOU'VE GOT IT MADE

According to Quinoa, it all begins with awareness and choice. Many of her uninformed (and poorly raised?) cohort devour fistfuls of goldfish crackers without even thinking of the social consequences. Quinoa's simple "Eat this, not that" approach can make all the difference. She printed out the following table on her letterpress as a handy pocket guide for each of her fellow students.

EMPTY-IMAGE CALORIES	ON-TREND UPGRADE
Ham-and-cheese sandwich	Prosciutto-and-brie panini with fig chutney
White rice	Mushroom and sage risotto
Macaroni and cheese	Panko-crusted white cheddar penne
Chicken nuggets	Lamb-shank lollipops with mint pesto
Mashed potatoes	Smashed red bliss potatoes with cracked black pepper and chives
Cheese and crackers	Goat cheese crostini with charred nectarines
Fruit snacks	Dark chocolate-covered pomegranate seeds with cayenne pepper
Buttered popcorn	Puffed couscous with herbed butter and sea salt
French fries	Roasted taro-root wedges with chipotle-horseradish dipping sauce
Mayonnaise	Garlic aioli
Applesauce	Jicama slaw with green apples and elderberries
Potato chips	Kale chips with almond butter and miso
Cheese pizza	Parmesan flatbread with roasted fennel
Oreos	Lavender and rosewater macarons

Part 2

HYPHENATE YOUR WAY TO GREAT

Quinoa says one of the best ways to ensure a solid, socially acceptable food choice is to opt for hyphenated items on the menu. She urges her beginning reader friends to search for that little black line and think of it as a springboard to culinary coolness. For example, plain butter is forgettable and bad for you, but Quinoa says chive-butter is on-trend and exciting. Strawberry jam is one of the most boring condiments of all time, but tomato-onion jam is completely on-point. Other hyphenated food words Quinoa endorses:

FETA-STUFFED

BALSAMIC-DRIZZLED

PEPPER-CRUSTED

PROSCIUTTO-WRAPPED

VEGAN-INSPIRED

GRASS-FED

PINEAPPLE-CHIPOTLE

WASABI-MAYO

YOGURT-DILL

CILANTRO-LIME

MAPLE-FIG

MANGO-CHILI

CURRY-DUSTED

ROSEMARY-GARLIC

SPINACH-KALE

PINEAPPLE-CUCUMBER

ANCHO-HONEY

SHAVED-COCONUT

AGAVE-SWEETENED

DAIRY-FREE

GLUTEN-FREE

BELIEVING THAT
THERE IS NO
FREEDOM IN *FREE
RANGE*, QUINOA
IS PROUD TO HAVE
STARTED THE FIRST
UNDERGROUND
CHICKEN
RAILROAD.

NOTHING
BOTHERS
QUINOA
MORE THAN
SOMEBODY
TRYING TO
PASS OFF
NONORGANIC,
UNSWEETENED
OAT MILK
FOR THE REAL
THING.

Part 3

EASY TO PRONOUNCE?
LESS THAN ONE OUNCE!

Finally, Quinoa stresses the importance of incorporating lots of exotic and multisyllabic foods into your diet. A quick rule of thumb: If the food is easy to pronounce or you are able to read its name aloud for the first time without mistakes, eat it sparingly—it's not likely to gain you any street cred.

Those who have completed Quinoa's program have experienced a minimum 75 percent increase in playdate invitations and expensive private school brochure mailings. One pleased mother reported that her son had a worrisome ketchup habit before Quinoa's intervention, but now he is absolutely flourishing with tamarind paste, garam masala, and Sriracha.

What's next for everybody's favorite two-foot foodie, you might be wondering?

QUINOA IS NOT AMUSED. APPARENTLY SOMEBODY THOUGHT IT WAS OKAY TO TAKE A SLICE OF CAKE BEFORE SHE INSTAGRAMMED IT.

Quinoa is already planning next year's curriculum: Oh, Snap! Properly Commemorating Your Meals on Instagram.

FOOD FOR THOUGHT: WHY EAT A CARROT WHEN YOU CAN EAT AN ACCESSORY?

Mondrian Sandwich

This incredible-looking sandwich, based on the timeless art of
Dutch painter Piet Mondrian, is one of Quinoa's favorites for lunch.
It's best paired with a black-and-white or color-blocked outfit.

1 SLICE EXPENSIVE RYE BREAD
(PREFERABLY ORGANIC,
VEGAN, OR GLUTEN-FREE)

1 SLICE CREAM
HAVARTI CHEESE

1 SLICE VERMONT
CHEDDAR CHEESE

1 HEIRLOOM
CHERRY TOMATO

1 LEAF ORGANIC
ROMAINE LETTUCE

1 TABLESPOON
HOMEMADE
HERB AIOLI

PARCHMENT PAPER
WASHI TAPE (RED, WHITE, BLACK, YELLOW, OR GREEN IN PATTERN)

QUINOA COULDN'T BE MORE PROUD OF HER FRIENDS PARSLEY AND STEVIA. BETWEEN THE THREE OF THEM, THEY INDIVIDUALLY LICKED EACH PIECE OF PRODUCE TO PROVE THAT THEIR FARM STAND IS PESTICIDE-FREE.

QUINOA'S *Twenty Tips* FOR
IMPROVING YOUR PERSONAL FOODIE STATUS

1. True foodies never pay a reasonable amount for anything they eat. Reasonably priced food is a major red flag. Look for any place with at least four dollar signs on Yelp!

2. Before going out with new friends, use the Applebee's Test to assess their foodie factor. If they have eaten at Applebee's anytime within the last five years, casually mention that you must terminate the friendship.

3. The only thing that makes good food taste better is waiting at least ninety minutes in line for it.

4. Post photos of your receipts from especially exclusive restaurants and simultaneously brag and complain about the high cost.

5. When it comes to chain restaurants, express frequently that you would rather die of starvation than eat at one, and have this written into your living will.

6. Look for opportunities to interject the terms *mouthfeel, earthy,* and *locavore* into food-centric conversations.

7. Have a lot of food-centric conversations with other foodies, peppered with plenty of inside jokes such as being pro-antipasti.

8. Float rumors that you're thinking of becoming a professional sommelier.

9. Carry reusable shopping bags and look down on those who don't.

FOOD FOR THOUGHT: WHY EAT A CARROT
WHEN YOU CAN EAT AN ACCESSORY?

10. Never eat anything that hasn't been properly Instagrammed first.

11. Practice saying *charcuterie* in the bathroom mirror one hundred times each morning.

12. Express disappointment as often as you can about how hard it is to find a good falafel.

13. Keep a food journal and read it to others.

14. Have a very specific order for your coffee and ensure that no barista can get it right, ever.

15. Refer to various lettuces exclusively as "greens" and comment on the nuanced flavors of them.

16. Talk about your favorite seasons and episodes of *Top Chef* and ask for boxed sets for your birthday.

17. Have strong preferences concerning bottled and sparkling waters and express those preferences.

18. Complain about how Williams-Sonoma has become suburban and boring.

19. Refuse to eat a hamburger unless it costs more than $14.

20. Overpronounce words like *parmigiano reggiano, marinara,* and *prosciutto.*

IT'S EASY
TO MEASURE
HOW
ANNOYED
QUINOA
IS BY THE
SIZE AND
FREQUENCY
OF HER
BUBBLES.

FOOD FOR THOUGHT: WHY EAT A CARROT
WHEN YOU CAN EAT AN ACCESSORY?

EVERY TIME CHEVRON FORGETS TO WEAR HER MATCHING BFF PEEP-TOE SHOOTIES, QUINOA REQUIRES HER TO PRODUCE FIFTEEN ORGANIC CARROTS. OTHERWISE, HOW WILL SHE EVER LEARN?

Chapter 8

QUINOA and CHEVRON, **BEST FRIENDS FOREVER** (PROBABLY)

Never one to leave anything to chance, Quinoa says her friendship with Chevron was a deliberate endeavor from the start. Her early precociousness indicated that she was born for greatness and would therefore need someone special in a best supporting role to serve as a playmate and confidant throughout her formative years. Someone who would photograph well, yet also shy away from Quinoa's spotlight. Someone who would work nicely into a future memoir and film option as a compelling character, yet never steal a scene. Basically, someone who would gladly serve as the wind beneath Quinoa's ever-widening wings.

Paired by a celebrity friendship matchmaker who uses a complex algorithm based on Apgar score, socioeconomic factors, bone structure, pedigree, design sensibility, and IQ, Chevron was selected as the likeliest BFF when the girls were only two months old. Chevron's solid-eight looks and mild manner were a perfect fit for Quinoa right from the start.

Of course, this arrangement wasn't one-sided. Chevron's parents were also seeking an ideal friend for their little darling, someone who might inspire the

SOME BFFS ARE JOINED AT THE HIP, BUT QUINOA AND CHEVRON ARE ALSO JOINED AT THE ELBOW, THE SHOULDER, AND THE PARIETAL LOBE. SO, THERE.

best in her and help draw her out of her natural introversion, which was already manifesting itself at three weeks old.

The girls' special chemistry was evident from their very first playdate (a Sunday brunch with a themed monochromatic dessert table and matching bunting): Quinoa remembers pulling a sterling silver Tiffany baby rattle from Chevron's grip to which

Chevron responded with squeals of delight. It was a match made in heaven!

Today, Quinoa and Chevron go together like rich kids and gluten sensitivity. Quinoa says they can spend hours and hours together playing haute couture dress-up, modern art installation, Leibovitz photo shoot, or just listening to Quinoa recite monologues from vintage Olsen

DURING THE IMPROMPTU PHOTO SHOOT, EVERYONE WAS CHEERING AND SHOUTING FOR QUINOA AND CHEVRON, EVEN THE PEOPLE FLAILING IN THE WATER.

FOR SOME REASON, BY THE TIME CHEVRON HAULS ALL THE BOOKS AND BLANKETS AND VINTAGE SUITCASES TO QUINOA'S READING NOOK, SHE ACTS TOO TIRED TO READ ALOUD.

twin films. While Chevron worships Quinoa (literally, at a makeshift shrine in her bedroom, a gift from Q), Quinoa feels her loving but mild disapproval of Chevron is the generous motivating force that will help her BFF achieve her fullest potential.

But, like any long-term relationship, Quinoa and Chevron have had their share of difficulties. There was the time Chevron said she didn't want to be the rabbit anymore when they played cosmetics testing. Or when Quinoa found out that Chevron secretly preferred *online* shopping. And, of course, there was the bad perm incident, of which Quinoa had explicitly warned Chevron about the potential risks. That experience, however, eventually brought the girls closer as they faced it together.

At the beginning, Quinoa coached Chevron to keep her head high and be bigger than the bad

IF QUINOA AND HER FRIENDS WANT TO HAVE A BEACH PARTY, THEY WILL HAVE A BEACH PARTY. AND NO AMOUNT OF TURF OR LANDLOCKED FORESTATION WILL STOP THEM.

DIDN'T YOU HEAR? QUINOA SAYS REAL BFFs EXCHANGE TRESS MESSAGES INSTEAD OF TEXT MESSAGES.

perm. But, as Chevron's suffering increased, Quinoa took matters into her own hands and gave the wild tresses a trim. Both girls wept throughout, and Quinoa describes the experience now as one of the most difficult moments of her young life, summoning bravery she didn't know she had and doing what had to be done. For a friend.

As Quinoa always says, what doesn't kill you makes you stronger, and her bond with Chevron today is stronger than ever. The girls enjoy a model friendship, in terms of both strength and photogenic quality. Quinoa says they can practically read each other's minds at this point, often choosing the same cupcake flavor at Sprinkles and the same glittered nail polish for their ring fingers at the manicurist. (If not on the first try, almost always on the second.)

What does the future hold for this friendship? The algorithm predicts success as long as Chevron's BMI doesn't stray too far off course, but only time will tell. Right now Quinoa and Chevron certainly have all the important makings of lifelong compatriots. If only today's marriages could be so well matched!

AS THE SAYING GOES, THE FRIENDS WHO FAUX-HAWK TOGETHER STAY TOGETHER.

BEING A BFF
MEANS BEING
BRUTALLY HONEST;
THEREFORE,
QUINOA WAS
OBLIGATED TO
POINT OUT THAT
CHEVRON'S
SHRUB WORK
WAS COMPLETELY
OUT OF SCALE,
AND THE PAWS
WERE CRUDELY
ASYMMETRICAL.

How Does Your BFF Score
on a Scale from 1 to **CHEVRON?**

QUINOA HAS TEN IMPORTANT QUESTIONS FOR YOU:

1. Does your friend have an interesting and memorable name that sounds good with yours?

2. Would your friend give you the shirt off her back, and, more importantly, would you want that shirt?

3. Does your friend enjoy doing whatever you want to do all the time?

4. Is your friend able to freely and frequently say, "I'm sorry," "You were right," and "I never should have doubted you"?

5. Does your friend look great (but not better than you)?

6. Does your friend know how lucky she is to have you as a best friend?

7. Do you and your friend share the same shoe size?

8. Does your friend let you solve all her problems and appreciate your unsolicited advice?

9. Does your friend's family secretly wish you were theirs instead?

10. If a better, more compatible friend came along, would your friend relinquish her spot out of love for you?

SCORING

8–10 YES RESPONSES: Your BFF is practically Chevron herself! (But it had better not be Chevron if she knows what's good for her!)

6–7 YES RESPONSES: Your friend shows potential, but don't buy her birthday gift too far in advance.

1–5 YES RESPONSES: Something is seriously wrong with her. Or you. Perhaps both of you.

QUINOA'S *Tips*
for *INCREASING YOUR FRIENDSHIP DRAMA*

Need to spice things up in your best friendship? Quinoa says a little drama can go a long way! Remember, though: For maximum results, you must profusely renounce drama while simultaneously creating it!

1. START VAGUE RUMORS ABOUT HER.
2. MEDDLE IN HER RELATIONSHIPS.
3. QUESTION HER LOYALTY.
4. DELIBERATELY MISUNDERSTAND HER.
5. START A TWITTER WAR WITH HER.
6. GO OLD-SCHOOL AND STAB HER IN THE BACK.
7. REVEAL HER SECRETS.
8. PULL HER HAIR AND CLAW AT HER EYES.

IMPORTANT NOTE:

Quinoa does not encourage or condone drama. In fact, Quinoa hates drama. She's just so sick of all the drama these days. Quinoa would like to rid the world of drama. She'd like to develop a drama cure and force everyone to drink it. Quinoa is a no-nonsense, no-drama girl who just wants to hang out with her BFF and have fun. Why does there always have to be so much drama, anyway? Who is causing all the drama? Who does these things? Who says that? Who are these people? Drama is the worst. Quinoa hates drama; she just absolutely hates it. She does. She hates drama so bad.

ALWAYS THE VIGILANT FRIEND, QUINOA NEVER FORGETS TO CHANGE CHEVRON'S ORDER TO LOW-FAT.

DESPITE HASHTAG'S COOL EXTERIOR, QUINOA ALWAYS HAS THE FEELING THAT HE IS RUNNING FROM SOMETHING.

Chapter 9

PLAYDATES *are the* NEW
POWER LUNCH

Many people today are over-whelmed by the vast amount of written and unwritten rules concerning modern playdates. For example, how do you ask someone on a playdate? Who pays? How many caterers are needed? What's an appropriate amount of time between playdates? Is it necessary to have a photo booth? How do you spot a serial playdater? What's the minimum llama-to-child ratio?

First of all, Quinoa reminds you not to get too ahead of yourself in this process. After all, her epic, three-part, Roman-themed playdate wasn't planned in a day. (The personalized gilded crowns alone took nine months!) At some point, everybody is a rookie in this game, so

Quinoa urges you to learn from her wisdom and not bite off more than you can chew.

Putting yourself on the playdating market is a significant milestone in every tot's life and there's no magic age when one becomes ready. Quinoa's friend Epsom was eager to enter the scene at fourteen months old, then made a major faux pas by napping during his first play-date, right in the middle of the private David Blaine magic show. Needless to say, Epsom was in third grade before he saw the inside of a playroom again. Quinoa urges you to wait until you are sure you can handle the rigorous sched-ule of a playdate (and maybe keep a can of Red Bull on hand, just in case).

When that day finally arrives, Quinoa recommends that you follow a few simple tips to ensure that you get invited on a second playdate. For starters, you must dress according to the theme and you must look fabulous. Showing up in something nontheme-related is an obvious snub to the host and a fast track to the blacklist. If you're invited to a Glamazon Rainforest playdate, you'd better show up in head-to-toe sequins and ethereal fairy wings.

During the playdate, come on strong, work the crowd, and mention how much money your parents make. One time Quinoa attended an Architecture & Arugula playdate at the Guggenheim where two of the children sat in the corner playing with blocks the *entire* time. Meanwhile, Quinoa closed two real estate

QUINOA LOVES THE DREAMY LOOK AIOLI GETS IN HIS EYES WHEN SHE TALKS ABOUT CASHMERE BLENDS.

THOUGH SHE APPRECIATED ALL HIS ATTENTION TO DETAIL ON THEIR PLAYDATE, QUINOA COULDN'T HELP BUT CALL DOWNTON OUT ON HIS FAKE ACCENT.

QUINOA HAD TO GIVE HIM AN A FOR EFFORT, BUT TWEED'S RUSTIC OUTDOOR PLAYDATE REEKED OF RECESSION.

deals, signed a record contract, and picked up a hot stock tip.

When the time comes for you to host your own playdate, Quinoa recommends hiring a professional playdate planner, especially for your first time. One time her friend Gypsum's mom thought she could whip together a simple picnic play-date. From the horrific last-minute text message invitation to the crude white bread PB&Js, every detail was disastrous. People showed up in a whole range of disjointed casual wear, even denim! Luckily, Quinoa kept the crowd from turning into an angry mob by explaining that Gypsum's mom was born and raised in North Dakota.

WHILE SOME PEOPLE THINK HIS ARTWORK IS DEPRESSING, IT'S WARHOL'S CORDUROYS THAT REALLY GET QUINOA DOWN.

It's also very important to keep a budget in mind as you're planning a playdate, says Quinoa. Otherwise, costs can spiral out of control. Before you know it, two celebrity choreographers turns into three or four. A good rule of thumb is to plan on two weeks'

salary (pretax, of course) for the basic expenses of custom invitations, location scout, location, set design, catering, hair, makeup, photography, branded gift bags, and security.

Quinoa advises you to beware of serial playdaters, like her longtime frenemy Hashtag. You've heard about these guys: working the crowd, loading up on free mocktails, filling their messenger bags with extra party favors, and hawking them on eBay. Like many schmoozers before him, Hashtag seems to get himself invited to all the first-rate playdates, yet mysteriously hasn't ever hosted.

Armed with her tips and a little shrewd acumen, Quinoa guarantees that you will enjoy a robust and fruitful playdating career. Just remember: There's no crying in play-dates, and there certainly isn't any playing.

QUINOA SAYS YOU DON'T REALLY KNOW SOMEONE UNTIL YOU'VE SAT IN THEIR DRAWERS AND WORN THEIR ACCESSORIES.

QUINOA'S
RESPECTABLE

Elaborate Playdate Themes

HIP-HOP & HAUTE COUTURE

AN AFTERNOON WITH RYAN GOSLING

TOUR OF CHINESE DYNASTIC FASHION

ANGRY SILENCE & ANGORA SWEATERS

MASON JAR MANIA

SNACK TIME AT TIFFANY'S

MERYL STREEP APPRECIATION

CSI: PRESCHOOL

MIRRORS! MIRRORS! EVERYWHERE!

VINTAGE CARS, VINTAGE CLOTHES, VINTAGE GRAPE JUICE

QUINOA ALWAYS FEELS SO RELAXED AROUND HER FRIEND COULIS. SOMETIMES IT'S JUST NICE TO BE WITH SOMEONE WHO UNDERSTANDS SEERSUCKER THE WAY YOU DO.

TURN DOWN A SUBPAR INVITATION

With Quinoa's help, no one need suffer through a bad playdate. Watch for these red flags and kindly respond with a simple, "Thank you, but I'd rather stick needles in my eyes."

- ✓ NO DRESS CODE
- ✓ MENTION OF TRAMPOLINES, BICYCLES, OR LASER TAG
- ✓ FAIRY-TALE PRINCESS DRESS-UP
- ✓ WORDS *CASUAL* OR *SNEAKERS* INCLUDED ON THE INVITATION
- ✓ BYO ANYTHING
- ✓ CRAYON OR LEGO AFFILIATION
- ✓ RUMORS OF JUICE BOXES OR RAISINS ON THE MENU
- ✓ LOCATIONS WITH THE WORD *PLAYLAND*

QUINOA'S FRIEND ELLIPSES HAS THE MOVES LIKE JAGGER, THE SMARTS LIKE ZUCKERBERG, AND THE CURFEW OF A TWELVE-YEAR-OLD.

WHEN ASKED WHAT WAS
ON THE HORIZON, QUINOA
STARED AT IT AND SAID,
"MORE RUFFLES."

Chapter 10

QUINOA *GOES* GLOBAL

Like everyone, Quinoa sometimes feels as if the 144 interior walls of her home are closing in on her and she begins itching for a getaway. Plus, it doesn't seem fair that she should stay in one place; fabulous cities around the world deserve to have regular visits from Quinoa. Whether it's a quick weekend trip or a month-long vacay, Quinoa feels that travel is one of the most important ways a child can learn about the world, second only to gangsta rap music. Once every month or so, she spins her wheel of favorite destinations and packs her Louis Vuittons for a jaunt abroad.

Now because of Quinoa's severe allergy to tourists, she is unable to share specific details about where to stay and which restaurants and boutiques to frequent. (It's not that Quinoa doesn't appreciate others wanting to replicate her exact life, but, you know, the allergy thing.) However, she's happy to share some of her most valuable tips that apply to every destination, be it London, Paris, Monte Carlo, Rome, Sydney, Bali, or Montauk. Probably even poor people places, too!

The number-one travel mistake Quinoa notices is that most people grossly underpack. A good rule of thumb is to have one piece of luggage for every day you're away. One time Quinoa's friend Semolina joined her for a weekend in London and showed

YES, QUINOA WILL ACCEPT THE HONOR OF BEING YOUR PEOPLE'S FASHION QUEEN. AND NOW SHE WOULD LIKE TO GIVE YOU SOMETHING, TOO — THIS VERY SPECIAL POSE. YOU'RE WELCOME.

up with only one bag. She ended up wearing the same shoes and jacket all weekend. It was terribly sad. Quinoa thought about lending her some options, but decided Semolina needed to learn a lesson.

While private jets are always the preferred option, Quinoa suggests mixing it up from time to time and flying first class with the commoners. It keeps things real.

Establish loyalty among the hotel staff by making a series of demands, such as freshly ironed pillowcases, steamed hand towels on the hour, and (Quinoa's favorite) requesting an original bedtime story with turndown service.

According to Quinoa, lines are for lemmings. Walk straight to the front of any line and push your way in. Trample if you must, but always say, "Excuse me."

HIS HIGHNESS, PRINCE ROTINI, WAS TERRIBLY EMBARRASSED WHEN HE REALIZED HE SHOULD HAVE BEEN REFERRING TO QUINOA BY *HER* FORMAL TITLE, HER AWESOMESAUCE FIERCENESS.

OOPSIE.
QUINOA HAS
A BAD HABIT OF
ACCIDENTALLY
DROPPING
PEOPLE'S
PHONES INTO
THE OCEAN
WHEN THEY
AREN'T PAYING
ATTENTION
TO HER.

Anytime you're traveling with others, Quinoa recommends always being the last one ready. The last one ready is the most important person. Obvi.

Every trip deserves spectacular new shoes, but it can be tough for fellow travelers to appreciate them while sightseeing. Quinoa recommends drawing attention to your shoes by walking slowly and complaining about blisters.

Keep things fresh by constantly changing your mind about what you want to do. As someone who prides herself on being certain about everything in everyday life, Quinoa relishes indecision on her vacations.

Something is bound to go wrong on every trip, so instead of letting fate decide, Quinoa recommends taking the reins and causing a problem on your

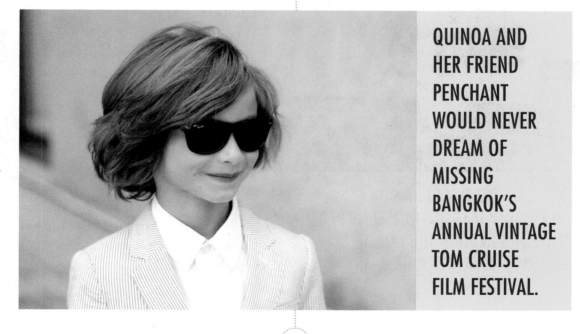

QUINOA AND HER FRIEND PENCHANT WOULD NEVER DREAM OF MISSING BANGKOK'S ANNUAL VINTAGE TOM CRUISE FILM FESTIVAL.

PROBABLY THE MOST COMMON FASHION MISTAKE QUINOA SEES WHEN TRAVELING AROUND THE WORLD IS NOT ENOUGH ALPACA HAIR.

own. Consider losing a train ticket, falsely accusing someone of theft, or accidentally shattering an artifact in a museum. The options are endless, but the point is to maintain control.

There's no need to learn another language, but Quinoa believes it's important to show respect for other cultures by speaking in their country's accent. Talk slowly and loudly in the presence of foreigners and they will be overwhelmed with gratitude.

To make room in your luggage for all the souvenirs and clothes you will purchase, Quinoa recommends throwing away all the clothes you brought on the trip. (As if you'd wear them again, anyway.)

More than anything, Quinoa reminds you that the purpose of a vacation is to relax, refresh, and rekindle your relationship with yourself. Those around you, from your travel companions to the strangers on the street, are there to nurture and support you along your way. Let them. Expect it. Demand it. The world will be a better place because of it.

HOW WILL QUINOA KNOW FOR SURE THAT THE HOTEL PILLOWS ARE 700 FILL EUROPEAN WHITE GOOSE DOWN IF SHE DOESN'T RIP A FEW OPEN, JUMP AROUND IN THEM, AND SEE FOR HERSELF?

QUINOA'S *Standard* PACKING LIST

FOR AN AVERAGE THREE-WEEK VACATION ABROAD, THIS LIST WILL HAVE YOU READY FOR EVERY POSSIBLE WARDROBE NEED.

- [ ] 2 leopard-print sweaters
- [ ] 6 shimmer-trim cardigans
- [ ] 3 cashmere crewneck cardigans
- [ ] 4 flutter-sleeved chiffon blouses
- [ ] 5 polka-dot, tiered, georgette blouses
- [ ] 6 peplum tops
- [ ] 4 organza blouses
- [ ] 3 dip-dyed fringe tanks
- [ ] 3 floral ruffle skirts
- [ ] 3 box-pleat tweed skirts
- [ ] 7 tulle skirts
- [ ] 3 sarong skirts
- [ ] 2 sequined shift dresses
- [ ] 4 silk racerback tank dresses
- [ ] 2 floral mesh dresses
- [ ] 3 chambray shirtdresses
- [ ] 2 paisley-print shift dresses
- [ ] 2 pintuck drop-waist dresses

- [ ] 4 brocade party dresses
- [ ] 3 color-block dresses
- [ ] 2 pair tuxedo pants
- [ ] 2 pair snakeskin skinny jeans
- [ ] 3 pair velvet floral jeans
- [ ] 3 pair satin quilted pants
- [ ] 3 pair houndstooth ombre shorts
- [ ] 5 crocheted swim cover-ups
- [ ] 3 kimono robes
- [ ] 4 pair silk pajamas
- [ ] 2 animal print, one-shoulder swimsuits
- [ ] 3 crocheted one-piece swimsuits
- [ ] 4 sequined two-piece swimsuits
- [ ] 5 tribal print caftans
- [ ] 4 rope belts
- [ ] 6 infinity scarves
- [ ] 36 beaded bangle bracelets
- [ ] 5 fedora hats

IT'S NOT IDEAL, BUT QUINOA AND BISCOFF HAVE FOUND A WAY TO MAKE JOINT CUSTODY OF THE ANGORA SCARF WORK FOR THEM.

- ☐ 6 sun hats
- ☐ 7 wool cloche hats
- ☐ 17 pair opaque tights
- ☐ 2 faux-fur shrugs
- ☐ 3 faux-fur vests
- ☐ 6 Aztec ponchos
- ☐ 3 floral-print jacquard coats
- ☐ 3 metallic leather bomber jackets
- ☐ 4 moto jackets
- ☐ 4 tweed jackets

- ☐ 3 bouclé blazers
- ☐ 2 pair crystal shaft flat boots
- ☐ 3 pair wedge strap boots
- ☐ 4 pair leather riding boots
- ☐ 3 pair sequined chukkah boots
- ☐ 3 pair distressed leather lace-up boots
- ☐ 6 pair ballet flats
- ☐ 3 pair metallic wedge shoes
- ☐ 4 pair studded flats
- ☐ 4 pair animal-print flats

QUINOA'S *Essential*
INTERNATIONAL PHRASES

KEEP ALL YOUR NEEDS MET WHEREVER YOU ROAM BY LEARNING
THESE LIFESAVING PHRASES IN OTHER LANGUAGES.

"IT'S A PLEASURE TO MEET ME."

"YES, I AM THE ONE YOU'VE BEEN HEARING ABOUT."

"BRING ME A FRESHLY BAKED PASTRY BEFORE MY BLOOD SUGAR DROPS ANY LOWER."

"I'LL TAKE ONE OF EVERYTHING."

"THIS FOOD DOES NOT MEET MY EXPECTATIONS. PLEASE HAVE THE CHEF FIRED."

"CAN YOU PLEASE REMOVE THESE TOURISTS FROM THE AREA?"

"RUB MY FEET."

"I'M GOING TO NEED YOU TO SPEAK ENGLISH."

"DOES THIS ANCIENT ARTIFACT COME IN BLUE?"

"HERE, DRIVER. PLEASE TAKE THIS DEODORANT. AND USE IT."

QUINOA NEVER TRAVELS WITHOUT HER PAPARAZZI DISGUISE: FRINGED OTTOMAN, WOOL SOCKS, HEAD TOWEL, AND FOREIGN TABLOID.

PHOTO CREDITS

pp. 10, 18, 39, 45, 52, 64, 72, 75, 111, 117, 123:
Lee Clower | leeclower.com

pp. 22, 30, 48, 57, 69: Jen Carver |
jencarverphotography.com | Designer: Joyfolie.com

p. 36: Jen Carver | jencarverphotography.com |
Designer: lillagrey.com

pp. 71, 78, 94, 116: Jen Carver |
jencarverphotography.com | Designer: Jakandpeppar.com

pp. 84, 92: Jen Carver | jencarverphotography.com |
Designer: lisasminimadhattery.com

p. 85: Jen Carver | jencarverphotography.com |
Designer: lofficielenfant.com

p. 114 and back cover: Jen Carver |
jencarverphotography.com |
Designer: Mustardpieclothing.com

pp. 8, 13, 15, 20, 33, 43, 67, 88, 95, 97, 100, 103, 107,
110, 118: Allie Cottrill | allisoncottrillphotography.com

pp. 6, 79, 83: Kelsey Foster | kelseyfoster.net

p. 14: Keight Dukes | putapuredukes.com

pp. 9, 55, 61, 76, 91 and front cover, 106, 119: Gina
Kim | ginakimphotography.com

pp. 25, 46, 80, 109, 121: Maxine Helfman Photography
| maxinehelfman.com (special thanks to Campbell Agency,
Kim Dawson Agency, and Wallflower Management)

p. 56: Karolina Henke / Skarp Agent |
skarp.se/karolina-henke

pp. 12, 54, 113: JaTawny Muckelvene Chatmon |
jatawnymchatmon.com

pp. 59, 104: Noreen Kidwai | Designer: noreenkidwai.com

pp. 17, 21, 29, 35, 44, 47, 60, 98, 99, 112, 120:
Alix Martinez Photography for PetiteParade |
petiteparade.com

pp. 32, 42, 66, 68, 125: Alix Martinez Photography |
alixmartinez.com

pp. 37, 40, 58, 70: Tabitha Patrick Photography for
BrasiLee Boutique | tabithapatrickphotography.com |
etsy.com/shop/BrasiLeeBoutique

p. 51: Marko Morelli | marko-morelli.com

p. 26: Brianne Wallace, Fleur + Dot Handmade
Childhoods | etsy.com/shop/FleurandDot

pp. 34, 96, 108: Nicola Toon |
hulahoopphotography.com | Designer (p.34): The Hateur
Hatter, hateurhatter.com

pp. 86, 87: Tiffany Beveridge

p. 15 (glasses): Thinkstock/Nastco

p. 16: Thinkstock/Ruben Pinto, Thinkstock/Nastco,
Thinkstock/aopsan, Thinkstock/habari1

p. 28: Thinkstock/Yougen

ACKNOWLEDGMENTS

This book, which took about nine months to produce, is very much my baby, but couldn't have happened without incredible key people in my life. Thanks to my agent, Allison Hunter, who helped Quinoa find the right home at Running Press, and to my editor, Jordana Tusman, and book designer, Ashley Haag, for making this book as smart and beautiful as Quinoa would demand.

Thanks to the incredible photographers: Lee Clower, Jen Carver, Allie Cottrill, Marko Morelli, JaTawny Chatmon, Maxine Helfman, Tabitha Patrick, Gina Kim, Nicola Toon, Kelsey Foster, Karolina Henke, and Alix Martinez, and designers Noreen Kidwai, Brianne Wallace, Keight Dukes, and Lee Brasile, who were all so generous with their work and without whom Quinoa could not exist in this form; and to every one of the beautiful models and their parents who added their support.

Thanks to my brother Jesse Crowley and dear friend Lauren Vaughn for their brilliant design work and head shot. Thanks to Ann Cannon, Allie Hagan, and Bunmi Laditan for offering sage advice, and to all the loyal readers and pinners who launched me into this opportunity. Thanks to Keith Coe for being a trusted friend and advisor, and to my dear friends Marianne and Mike Strong, Susan and Erik Vaughn, Estelle and Stan Lukoff, Mina and Dave Sorensen, Kirsten and Bart Slaugh, and Beth Morling, who have offered a constant chorus of support.

Thanks to my entire Crowley and Beveridge families for unending love and support, and especially to Andrea Peterson who publicized me to every hair client through her door. A special shoutout to my lifelong friends of the Would-Be Writers Guild too.

Finally, to my greatest treasures, my sons Christian and Max. And to my husband Ryan, my moon, my mainstay, my everything: You've given me the best life imaginable.

Tiffany Beveridge is a freelance copywriter who has written everything from consumer catalogs to radio ads for national brands such as Mrs. Fields Cookies, DuPont, and Benjamin Moore. An avid blogger, tweeter, Facebooker, and pinner, Tiffany lives with her husband and two wonderful (but averagely dressed) sons outside Philadelphia, PA.

Find Quinoa on Pinterest at My Imaginary Well-Dressed Toddler Daughter and on Twitter at @ImaginaryQuinoa.